LIVERPOOL

City Beautiful

LIVERPOOL
City Beautiful

David Cottrell

LIVERPOOL
1207~2007

breedon **books**
PUBLISHING

First published in Great Britain in 2007 by
The Breedon Books Publishing Company Limited
Breedon House, 3 The Parker Centre, Derby DE2I 4SZ.

All photography by the author.

ISBN 978-1-85983-591-3

Printed and bound by Cromwell Press,
Trowbridge, Wiltshire.

CONTENTS

For my dad, Stan the man

Introduction

'A city is the greatest of the works of art; written on its walls are the tradition and the history of the past, outlined in its composition is the imprint of the human soul'
Stanley Adshead, University of Liverpool professor of civic design, 1912–1914

The sun sets opposite Liverpool's Pier Head, so that its three magnificent Graces are bathed in lingering light at the end of a fine day, while all over town long shadows are cast upon some of the most impressive buildings in the country. Like dawn, this is a good time to appreciate the wealth of architecture and public sculpture in a city granted World Heritage Site status in 2004.

Ask anyone in a Liverpool street to rattle off half-a-dozen great buildings – their own buildings – and straightaway, probably, they'll name the three at the Pier Head, the two cathedrals, St George's Hall and the Albert Dock. These are merely the icing on the cake. Liverpool has 2,500 listed properties, including 26 Grade I – more than any other city outside London – and most of them are condensed into a relatively small area, from the late Georgian terraces and red-brick academia around Hope Street, via the neoclassical splendour of William Brown Street, to the palatial offices and mighty functionalism of the business district and waterfront.

Again, only the capital surpasses Liverpool for public sculpture. The city is a microcosm of British taste in sculpture over the ages: from the conventional bronze commemorative statues of Victorian times, when tens of thousands of people would turn out for the unveiling ceremonies, to the more symbolic art and architectural decoration in the first half of the 20th century, expressed through war memorials and even the decorative iron gates of public houses.

A century ago, upon the eve of a second great wave of building, Liverpool staged a high-profile urban-planning conference entitled City Beautiful, which debated how the architecture, particularly along the waterfront, affected its appearance to natives and visitors alike. With a plethora of neoclassical and Gothic architecture – teeming with carved ornament – already in place, what could be next? The answer was a a swathe of simple but monumental new buildings, creamy white in colour and colossal in scale, exemplified by the Martins Bank Building on Water Street, the Cunard Building on the Pier Head and the Adelphi Hotel at Ranelagh Place.

Sculpture evolved, too. After the Victorian obsession with civic pride came an explosion of rich and expresssive architectural decoration in the early 1900s, often executed by graduates from the city's prolific School of Architecture. This bridge to the post-war era was signified by Jacob Epstein's Liverpool Resurgent on the Lewis's department store, as well as a flurry of abstract steel and concrete creations in and around the university's precincts.

This book not only celebrates Liverpool's 800th birthday, but marks the centenary of the original City Beautiful conference and its gift of a handsome, harmonious cityscape bequeathed by shrewd, urbane custodians to future generations. The current flourish of new-build activity – not least Grosvenor's massive Liverpool One project, the arena and convention centre at Kings Waterfront, the thriving Princes Dock and soon, perhaps, the vast, undeveloped Central Docks – is the first since the early 20th century.

Today's challenge is to enhance rather than destroy the existing urban fabric, make an equally lasting impression and embrace the spirit of the bold, theatrical and daring architecture for which Liverpool was once famous. For now, from the banks and warehouses to the museums and galleries, and the public sculpture at all points inbetween, spare a moment to enjoy some glorious reminders as the city's current renaissance continues apace, of an era when Liverpool truly ruled the waves.

ANGEL

A marble angel (left) commemorating Agnes Jones, a nurse at the city's Brownlow Hill workhouse in the mid 1800s, resides inside the Oratory, a miniature Greek temple in the grounds of the Anglican Cathedral designed by John Foster Junior. Below and bottom, angels on the façade of another fine example of Greek Revival architecture, the old Wellington Rooms on Mount Pleasant, designed by Edmund Aikin in 1816. Right, a bronze figure of an angel watches over St John's Gardens behind St George's Hall.

ARCADE

Secreted in Queen Avenue and accessed via an archway on Dale Street or narrow passageway off Caste Street, is one of Liverpool's best examples of Greek Revival architecture. Dating from 1837, the Royal Bank was the work of Samuel Rowland, who also designed the dazzlingly white Church of St Bride on Percy Street. It has two types of columns: simple Doric (see Wellington's Column) and Ionic (scrolls either side of the capital – see the Oratory). Among the courtyard's other gems are carved seashells, period lamp standards and iron gates.

13

BANK

Rows of noble office buildings stand testament to Liverpool's rich banking heritage, which was founded upon maritime commerce. Dating from the late Victorian period, their styles vary from the neoclassical Bank of England (below) to the French Renaissance Leyland & Bullins Bank (left) and Adelphi Bank (right). Overleaf are the Premier Buildings (now Lloyds Bank) at the corner of Hanover Street and Church Street, and the former First National Bank on James Street. These are two examples of the Liverpool Manner in the early 20th century: robust buildings with grey masonry, symmetrical columns and iron balconies.

If ever a building epitomised Liverpool's financial swagger in the first half of the last century, it's the Martins Bank that fronts on to Water Street and overlooks the Town Hall. Designed by Herbert Rowse (the architect behind the India Building, the Philharmonic Hall and the George's Dock Building) for a bank with 560 branches worldwide by the 1930s, it rises 150ft above ground level and is set back in successive planes at the levels of neighbouring roofs. There are nine floors above ground level, plus a mezzanine and three below, with its foundations 50ft under the building. Roughly rectangular in shape, it's 180ft in length and over 140ft wide.

BREWERY

When smoke billows from the tall chimney of the Cains Brewery at the corner of Stanhope Street and Grafton Street, there's a definite aroma of fermenting hops and barley in the air. It is those very ingredients that appear in terracotta (below) upon the red-brick façade of this grand building, along with heraldic arms featuring a harnessed unicorn and the Latin motto Pacem Amo, meaning 'I Love Peace' (left). Incidentally, the same legend – this time accompanied by two unicorns – reappears upon the wrought-iron gates of the Philharmonic Hotel on Hope Street. Founded by Irishman Robert Cain, the brewery was acquired by Higsons in 1923, closed in 1990 and then reopened under the original Cains name in 2002.

BUILDING

Within the fairly concentrated and walkable area of Liverpool's city centre is a rich variety of architectural styles, shades and textures, with civic, commercial, religious and academic buildings closely juxtaposed. Nos. 17–19 Church Street (left) is a stunningly attractive but often overlooked ensemble of red bricks and round arches by Herbert Rowse, from

1930. The much earlier Berey's Building (below) at the corner of Bixteth Street and Ormond Street adds sandstone to its Gothic mix, while G. & F. Holme's sturdy Hahnemann Hospital on Hope Street (right) has elements of terracotta and Welsh grey slate. Overleaf is the icing-sugar ornamentation of Victoria Chambers on Castle Street.

No. 16 Cook Street (left) resembles a giant church window minus the stained glass, like a huge pane with three arches divided by slender stone mullions. It was built in 1866 to the specifications of Peter Ellis and today it's regarded as a modernist icon, as it predates the same kind of glazed commercial structures in America by a good two decades. The

Hargreaves Building (bottom left) on Chapel Street and the Fowlers Building on Victoria Street (pages 32 and 33) are typical Victorian offices by James Picton, an architect inspired by Venetian palaces. Half a century later, the Beaux Arts found expression in the India Building (below), the Athenaeum (right) and the Adelphi Hotel (bottom right).

Previous pages: reclining female figures occupy the round-arched window bays of the Renaissance-style Masons Buildings (1866) on Exchange Street East. In sharp contrast is the imposing North Western Hotel on Lime Street (left), which is one of several Gothic Revival masterpieces in the city by Alfred Waterhouse (see his old Royal Infirmary at Pembroke Place, the University Victoria Building on Brownlow Hill, the Prudential Assurance Building on Dale Street, and also the Natural History Museum in London).

Amid the late-Georgian terraces of Percy Street it's back to the neoclassical in the shape of the Church of St Bride (below), while influences from several architectural genres constitute the University of Liverpool's Guild of Students on Mount Pleasant (right) – a small-scale tour de force by celebrated professor of architecture Charles Reilly in 1913.

CAT

A tiger bares its impressive fangs on the great bronze doors of the old National & Provincial Bank on Water Street. The teeth were ritually rubbed by visiting Lascars (Indian and South East Asian sailors) for good luck. Below there is one of a pride of four huge lions, each 14ft long, standing guard at St George's Plateau. And on the right are twin lion heads in Portland stone on the parapet of the Woolworths Building on Church Street.

CEILING

Classical heads and torsos emerge, dreamlike, from the ceiling of the magistrates room in County Sessions House (below). On the near right are cherubs on the ceiling of the dining room at 19 Abercromby Square, once the home of a South Carolina businessman based in Liverpool during the American Civil War (one is astride a wild turkey, the state's game bird). On the far right is the fabulous barrel-vaulted arcade of the India Building on Water Street.

CEMETERY

Butterflies often flit over the stone, lichen and ivy, and in the hush an ancient spring trickles along the eastern wall of St James's Cemetery in the shadow of the Anglican Cathedral. A few feet away, carved into the bare rock, are the initials J.C. and the date 1876. In the north-east corner of the cemetery, someone with a craftsman's flair has chiselled 'AS 1727' into the rockface, which has been scoured with striations left by horse-drawn drays laden with quarried sandstone.

This vast man-made crater, hewn from the natural hill once known as Mount Zion, was converted into a burial ground when the sandstone was exhausted in 1825. Today it's still accessed via ramps and tunnels that its original designer, John Foster, lined with catacombs. Sons and daughters of Kentucky, South Carolina, New York, New Jersey, Massachusetts and Pennsylvania are buried here, and there are also many memorials to those that perished at sea. Here lies Sarah Biffin, born in 1784 and namechecked by Charles Dickens in Nicholas Nickleby. Only 37-inches tall and with no arms and legs, she became one of the most noted portrait artists of her day and was patronised by four monarchs. There is also Captain John Oliver, veteran of the battles of the Nile, Copenhagen and Trafalgar, who served under Lord Nelson on HMS *Victory*; William Huskisson, MP for Liverpool and the first man to be killed by a train (Stephenson's *Rocket* in 1832); and Kitty Wilkinson, who cared for the poor during the 1832 cholera epidemic.

SACRED to the MEMORY
of
DAVID KEAY,
who was drowned on his homeward
passage from Philadelphia to
Liverpool, 12th Septr 1834,
Aged 19 Years.

Also Captain JAMES KEAY, who
died at Africa 22nd June 1837,
Aged 28 Years.

Also THOMAS KEAY, who died
at Demerara 10th Novr 1839,
Aged 19 Years.

Also Captain ALEXANDER KEAY,
Father of the above, who died 25th June
1849, Aged 62 Years.

Blessed are they who die in the LORD."

CHERUB

Putti is the plural term for the representation of naked infants, especially winged cherubs or cupids, originating from Renaissance art and finding form as decorative sculpture upon Victorian architecture in Britain. They often appear in entablatures, friezes and reliefs over porticos and doorways, and they can be seen holding swags, banners and garlands of fruit and flowers upon the office buildings of Exchange Street East (below and bottom), blowing clarions upon the Guardian Assurance Building on Dale Street (near right), and clinging precariously to the pilasters of the old Adelphi Bank on Castle Street (far right).

CHIMNEY

From the bottom of Mount Pleasant, little Victorian
chimney pots crowd around the spectacular, glass and steel
stack of 'Paddy's Wigwam', otherwise known as the
Metropolitan Cathedral of Christ the King. Completed in
1967, it boasts the world's largest stained-glass window
in its Lantern Tower, which itself weighs 2,000 tons.
Rising 331ft, the central tower of the Anglican Cathedral
dominates the elegant rooftops of Percy Street (below
left) and the junction of Princes Road and Parliament Street
(below right). Completed in 1942, the tower
contains 13 bells with the heaviest and highest ringing peal
in the world. The entire cathedral was 100 years
old in 2004, although it took the best part of 75 years to
complete. Overleaf, a dozen slender chimney pots sit upon
the extravagant roof of 34–36 Castle Street, which were the
erstwhile offices of the Leyland & Bullins Bank.

45

CLOCK

Liverpool's most famous clockfaces are undoubtedly those upon the Royal Liver Building, but there are also other fine examples in the city, notably The Vines public house on Lime Street (left), the gilded sun dial of the old Royal Insurance Building on Dale Street (below), and the three faces at the former Exchange Station on Tithebarn Street. Arguably the most impressive of them all are the twin discs on the clocktower of the university's Victoria Building at the top of Brownlow Hill (bottom).

DOCK

The Albert Dock is not so much beautiful as noble and certainly heroic. Now over 160 years old, it's one of the earliest enclosed docks in the world, the largest group of Grade I listed buildings in England, and it is something akin to a waterfront castle. A triumph of function and design, it was conceived in 1846 by Jesse Hartley (the city's Dock Engineer) and consists of five formidable warehouses. Witness the sheer bulk of their sandstone and granite blocks – an oustanding example of irregular, cyclopean masonry – the enormous cast-iron columns lining the dock itself, and the gate piers like giant chess pieces at the corner entrances. Each warehouse stands five storeys high, and their combined capacity is 250,000 tons.

Around them, there are two other docks (Canning and Salthouse), a hydraulic pumping station, swing bridges, watchmen's huts and a pier master's house. The Albert Dock was almost demolished in the 1980s, yet today the area is one of the UK's biggest tourist attractions and a conservation site, housing museums, galleries, bars, restaurants, shops and apartments. Head south from here and you come, consecutively, to the docks of King's (dominated by the new Arena & Conference Centre), Wapping, Queen's, Coburg and Brunswick (home to Liverpool Marina). Together these southern docks represent a fifth of the city's UNESCO World Heritage Site officially inscribed in late 2004.

DOME

Six sentinels with gilded hair and wings (left) are perched upon the shallow cupola at the top of Renshaw Street, while there are some structural similarities between the domed Pembroke Place (below left) and the Royal Insurance Building (below right) on Dale Street. On the right, the Town Hall interior is inscribed with the city motto, and overleaf is the Byzantine dome of Central Hall (top left), one of the four smaller domes of the Port of Liverpool Building (bottom) and the Imperial Buildings on Whitechapel (right).

DOOR

To the left is Stanley Hall on Edmund Street. With gleaming brass on an authentic Art Deco frontage, it was formerly home to Silcocks grain merchants. Below are the twin tigers upon the National Provincial Bank of Water Street. Overleaf is the old Adelphi Bank on Castle Street, which has bronze doors depicting historical pairs of inseparable friends: Achilles and Patroclus (Greek warriors), Castor and Pollux (twin sons of Zeus), David and Jonathan (champions of Israel) and Roland and Oliver (knights of Charlemagne). Also pictured is the grand doorway of the Hargreaves Building on Chapel Street, designed by Victorian architect James Picton.

FACE

Along with the ubiquitous Liver Bird, nautical imagery like mermaids, dolphins and allegorical figures, representing the Mersey and the city itself, and countless sculpted heads from classical mythology line Liverpool's streets like ancient sentinels, mostly adorning buildings from the 19th century. Male and female, serene or severe, they wear crowns, helmets and garlands, and some – like Athena, Apollo, Neptune and Hermes – are more easily identifiable than others. On this page (clockwise from top): the Cunard Building, the University Faculty of Arts, the Hope Street Hotel and 1 Dale Street, and on the opposite page is the Adelphi Hotel. Pictured overleaf are: County Sessions House, the Cunard Building, the India Building, the George's Dock Building, 16 Cook Street, the Metropolitan Cathedral and the George's Dock Building again (these pharaonic faces on the Queensway Tunnel ventilation shaft symbolise night and day).

FAITH

Liverpool's pre-eminence as a port has attracted Irish, German, Greek, Italian, Polish, Swedish and Jewish communities, and with them places of worship. The city's first synagogue was founded in 1807 on Seel Street. Some 65 years later, at the height of Europe's fascination with Orientalism, one of the most beautiful synagogues in Anglo-Jewry was consecrated on Princes Road (right). On the Ullet Road Unitarian Church is a stained-glass window (left) by Edwards Burne-Jones and William Morris, and overleaf are the gates to the Anglican Cathedral.

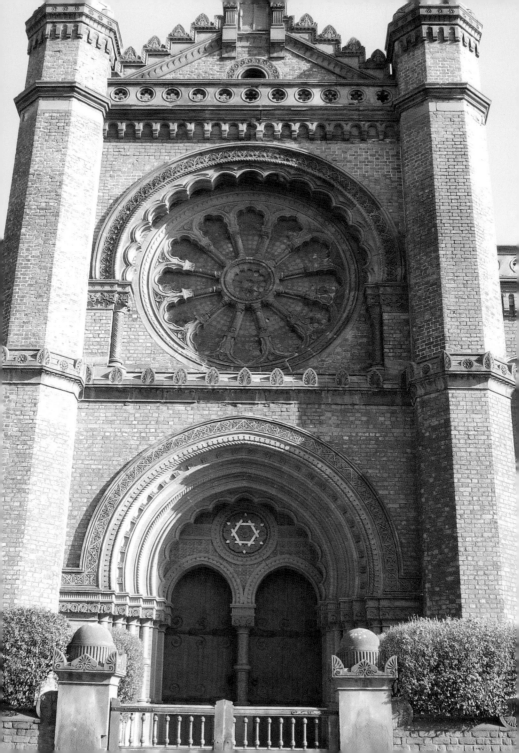

A statue of Christ upon a donkey (below left) is placed in the grounds of the Church of Our Lady and St Nicholas. Because the latter is also the patron saint of seamen, it's also known as the Sailor's Church. A more modernist personification stands high above the great entrance to the Anglican Cathedral (below right), while Christ also appears in the Last Supper (below) upon the Catharine Street façade of St Philip Neri's Church. On the right is St Luke's, or the 'Bombed-out Church' as locals call it. Dominating the top of Bold Street, it was completed in 1831 but damaged during World War Two, and it now stands as a monument to peace. Overleaf are views of the Metropolitan Cathedral, Frederick Gibberd's epitome of 1960s monumental concrete design, and its colossal Anglican counterpart at the opposite end of Hope Street – the fifth largest cathedral in the world.

FISH

Pictured below is a mosaic detail on the frontage of the former British & Foreign Marine Insurance HQ on Castle Street, and on the right a fish in stone upon the Port of Liverpool Building. On the far right, four fish sit at the base of lamp standards outside the old Technical College, now part of the World Museum on William Brown Street. And at the bottom is a fabulous octopus on the underside of a balcony on the Martins Bank Building on Water Street.

FLOOR

The mosaic flooring of the County Sessions House (left) is based upon a Romano-British design that was discovered at the time of the building's completion in the late 19th century. Below is the Town Hall's magnificent encaustic tiled floor featuring the city's coat of arms. And on the right is the Hippocratic oath as it appears upon the floor of the Liverpool Medical Institution (built in 1836 on Mount Pleasant), with twin serpents entwined around the staff of Asclepius, the Greek god of healing. The building also boasts a 17th-century grandfather clock, medical library and display of gruesome surgical instruments.

FOUNTAIN

Located between the entrance to the Walker Art Gallery and the Small Concert Room of St George's Hall, this cast-iron masterpiece was unveiled in 1877 as a gift to the city from its mayor, R.F. Steble. The figures around the base represent Neptune, Amphitrite (his wife), Acis (a river deity) and Galatea (sea nymph). It's a copy of an original designed by Paul Lienard for the Paris World Fair of 1855. There's another version outside Massachusetts State House in Boston as well as faithful replicas in Lyon, Bordeaux, Geneva and Cairo.

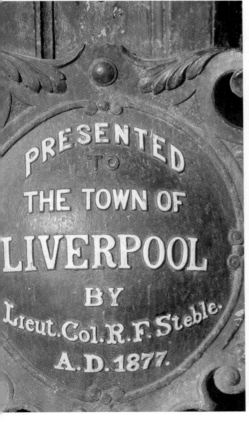

PRESENTED
TO
THE TOWN OF
LIVERPOOL
BY
Lieut.Col.R.F.Steble.
A.D.1877.

GALLERY

The exterior of the Walker on William Brown Street, opened in 1870 as the first major public art gallery outside London, illustrates 19th-century Liverpool's love affair with neoclassicism, combining Greek ideals of harmony with Roman advances in technology. Its portico (entrance bay) is a temple projecting from an ashlar (square-cut stone) façade. The pediment's elaborate cornice (top right) and the intricate frieze (middle) above the entrance are typical decorative devices dominated by six fluted Corinthian columns (bottom). Either side of these are seated statues of Michelangelo and Raphaell which represent sculpture and painting. Overleaf, the side elevation opposite County Sessions House has reliefs of King John Plantagenet granting the city's charter in 1207, Prince Rupert laying siege to Liverpool during the English Civil War, and Queen Victoria paying a visit in 1851. From the rear of the building, an allegorical personification of Liverpool with a Liver Bird at her side greets visitors to the gallery.

GRACES

At the iconic water's edge, the Pier Head is dominated by the familiar mirages of the Royal Liver, the Cunard and the Port of Liverpool Buildings, collectively known as the Graces after the three daughters of Zeus, who represent splendour, festivity and abundance. The Port of Liverpool Building (this page) was built in 1907 in the style of a Renaissance palace with a classical dome. The atrium floor has a compass motif, and near the Pier Head entrance is the signature of the Italian craftsman who oversaw the creation of the building's ornate marble flooring, currently being refurbished.

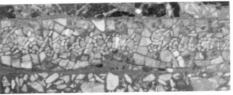

The third Grace was completed in 1916 for Cunard, the famous line founded by Samuel Cunard of Halifax, Nova Scotia, and George Burns and David MacIver, of Glasgow and Liverpool. Its first ship, the *Britannia*, had sailed to North America on 4 July 1840, and seven years later Cunard had established a weekly steam-packet service between Liverpool and New York.

The building takes the form of an Italian palazzo and is decorated with carved details of peoples from around the world, the crests of British ports and countries allied to Britain in World War One, signs of the zodiac and, at each corner, American eagles holding Cunard shields. It is Grade II listed and, like her sisters, built to last.

The Royal Liver Building is Grade I listed and up there with Big Ben as the most famous edifice in the country. Designed by Walter Aubrey Thomas and completed in 1911 as the new home for the Royal Liver Friendly Society, it stands 320ft high and occupies over an acre of land. The great copper birds were designed by German craftsman Carl Bernard Bartels. Inside is a monumental stained-glass window at the western end of the ground floor. It features a central figure representing Navigation and Commerce, standing on a landing stage and holding a mariner's chart and caduceus, with an anchor and capstan at her feet. Below her, Neptune emerges from a shell holding a trident, and elsewhere there are sea nymphs, dolphins, tridents, sextants and ancient and modern ships.

GREEN

The great swathes of Stanley, Newsham and Sefton Parks are a legacy from late Victorian days, when Liverpool's great and good had the foresight to create green lungs for a city seething with humanity. Earlier still, Liverpool boasted Botanic Gardens, which were opened at Mount Pleasant by man of letters William Roscoe in 1802. After a later spell at Edge Hill the collections were dispersed to Calderstones Park and Garston.

Today there remain lots of urban retreats like the John Moores University Garden off Maryland Street (right and far right), an oasis of new and old buildings framed by ivy-clad trees, and Abercromby Square (below), dating from 1800 and named after Ralph Abercromby (the general who defeated the French at Alexandria in Egypt) and formerly a garden for the merchants who lived in the surrounding terraces.

Pictured on the previous page is St John's Gardens, the sloping terrace behind St George's Hall, which was laid out as terraced gardens on a former church site 100 years ago and today features several monuments to the city's great and good. The magnificent sunburst gates at Princes Park (left) were designed by James Pennethorne, architect of the ballroom at Buckingham Palace and the capital's Kennington, Victoria and Battersea Parks. Further south there is Calderstones Park, whose Harthill entrance (below) is watched over by statues of the Four Seasons. And overleaf are pictures of winter, spring, summer and autumn in action at Sefton Park.

At around 1,000 years old Allerton Oak (left) in Calderstones Park is Liverpool's oldest living inhabitant, while the city's tallest trees are the beeches of Otterspool Park (right). Allerton Manor (below) is one of several ruined country houses in the leafy and once hugely-wealthy south Liverpool suburbs. Built for the ship-owning Fletchers and now in the middle of a golf course, only its old colonnade remains. Today Liverpool boasts one million trees and over 2,500 acres of parks and open spaces. Ten parks in the city have been awarded Green Flag status, while Chavasse Park is being re-landscaped as part of Grosvenor's Liverpool One retail project.

GULL

Wheeling, swooping, shrieking to a distant soundtrack of hydraulic bus brakes in the city centre, or occasionally just watching the human traffic from their roosts on ledges and rooftops. Liverpool without its seagulls is unthinkable.

LIVER BIRD

The world-famous symbol of Liverpool, a mythical hybrid of cormorant and eagle, appears upon countless buildings in and around the city centre, almost always depicted in profile with the customary sprig of seaweed in its bill. A well-groomed version stands in cartouches beneath each of the 30 ground-floor windows of the Martins Bank Building on Water Street (left), while opposite a golden bird with elevated wings (below) unusually faces right upon the old offices of the Liverpool Building Society. It appears in profile in discs at the base of the George's Dock Building on the Pier Head (top right) and three times upon the university's arms (bottom).

MERMAID

At 3–5 Castle Street, once home to the British & Foreign Marine Insurance Company, tiny pairs of mermaids with entwined tails, accompanied by shields containing anchors, can be seen upon the sandstone columns above the building's entrance. In the distinctive sculptural style of master carver Herbert Tyson Smith, mermaids run amok on the Martins Bank Building on nearby Water Street, supporting the bank's initial 'M' (below) and balancing cornucopias of spilling coins upon their shoulders (right). Note the latter's webbed fingers and graceful, swirling twin tails.

MONOLITH

From the narrow approach of Roe Alley (left), the Queensway Tunnel ventilation shaft on North John Street is Liverpool's equivalent of the ancient temple at Petra. Except this isn't Jordanian rock, it's Portland stone – cladding two of the six streamlined shafts designed by Herbert Rowse in the 1930s. Quarried for centuries from the eponymous peninsula in Dorset, Portland stone is a 200-million-year-old limestone famous for its capacity to absorb and reflect light. In bright sunshine, it dazzles. And carving it – say the experts – is like cutting into a block of light, even producing rhythmic soundwaves.

MONUMENT

Wellington's Column (left) on William Brown Street was erected 11 years after the duke's death in 1852, with a relief of Waterloo at the base. Legend has it that his bronze statue is cast from gunmetal salvaged from the battle. On the right is a detail from the bronze Post Room Memorial at Exchange Flags (1924). Pictured below is the war memorial at Hamilton Square in Birkenhead, sculpted by Herbert Tsyon Smith, who also worked upon the poignant yet strikingly futurist Cenotaph at St George's Plateau, which can be seen overleaf.

The Cunard war memorial (left) features a nude personification of Victory, striding on the prow of a Roman galley. On the bottom left, the Construction Workers' monument at Gerard Gardens behind the World Museum. And, bottom right, a skeleton emerges from a cloak upon Nelson's Monument, erected in 1813 to mark his death eight years earlier. Four shackled figures represent his victories over the French navy at Cape St Vincent, the Nile, Copenhagen and Trafalgar. Pictured on the right is one of four stone figures symbolising the elements 20ft up the obelisk-shaped memorial to the Engine Room Heroes near Princes Dock. Commemorative of 'those who keep the lights burning', who were originally the 32 engineers of the *Titanic*.

MOSAIC

Many of the beautiful mosaic entrance floors to Liverpool's finest office buildings and public houses were laid by terrazzo marble craftsmen from the Italian community that settled around Gerard Street in Vauxhall, just north of the city centre, in the late 19th century. On the left is the superb basement entrance to the City Vaults at 14 Cook Street. Pictured right is the mosaic floor leading into the Lion Tavern at the junction of Moorfields and Tithebarn Street. Below left is from the historic White Star pub on Button Street, originally a ships chandlers shop, and below right can be seen at a former apothecary on Castle Street, now occupied by a leather goods store.

MUSIC

The cubic exterior of the Philharmonic Hall on Hope Street, designed by the great Herbert Rowse in 1936 to replace an original building consumed by fire, has been described as 'frozen music'. Unlike his more conventional and monumental office blocks in the business district, this brick building fuses modernist style with acoustic data to create another landmark that he described as 'shaped like a megaphone with the orchestra at the narrow end'. Dutch architect W.M. Dudok has been cited as a major influence for the hall. Inside there are etched representations of musical notes and instruments in the shape of shipping vessels (below), as well as large-scale gilded reliefs of Apollo, Greek god of harmony (right) – all by Edmund C. Thompson, who, along with fellow craftsman George T. Capstick, supplied the carved sculptural decoration upon the George's Dock Building at the Pier Head and new Exchange Flags. Also inside there is a copper memorial to the musicians of the *Titanic*, which can be found by the main entrance. Rowse's initials, it's claimed, are woven into the concert hall's sumptuous carpets.

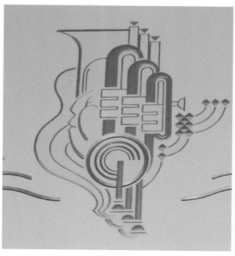
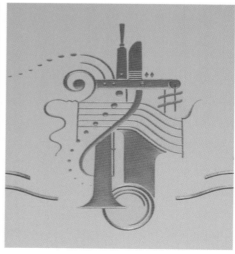

NEPTUNE

Carvings of the ancient god of the sea are almost as numerous as the Liver Birds upon Liverpool buildings. On a keystone above the Exchange Street East entrance to the old office of the Liverpool & London & Globe Insurance Company at 1 Dale Street (below), he wears a crown of tridents with dolphins swimming either side of his head. Upon the Cunard Building (middle top) open-mouthed fish sit above his own gills, while at 20 Sir Thomas Street (middle bottom) a simple crown rests above his deep, sunken eyes. High upon the roof of the former College of Commerce at 79 Tithebarn Street (far right), he looms like a figurehead from the prow of a rowing boat accompanied by more fish. Overleaf he can be seen inside a giant shell upon the India Building on Water Street (top left); with triton and dolphins upon the Martins Bank Building (middle); with coiled fishtails upon Victoria Chambers on Castle Street (bottom); and a comic-book caricature with beefcake physique, fin-like girdle and conch upon Spinney House on Church Street (far right).

125

NEW

Regeneration on a massive scale is juxtaposing old and new in 21st-century Liverpool. To the left is the bold blue façade of a new hotel at Old Haymarket. Pictured below, a gull glides past the 30-storey Beetham Tower, and on the right, the view looking back towards town – and the 'pod' at the top of the Unity scheme – from Princes Dock, where a slick design template incorporates a variety of textures and surfaces, like stainless steel and solar-tinted glass, to complement the calm waters and cobblestones of the dock environment.

Previous page: the arching water-jet fountain at Williamson Square is a recent addition to a popular public space that accommodates the legendary Playhouse Theatre. Inlaid around the fountain is a poem by Roger McGough, written to be read from any point 'Water is Liverpool is river is paradox.' The Faces of Liverpool peer from blue-glass portholes around Beetham Tower (left), celebrating the city's global connections, diverse culture and ethnic mix with images of its contemporary residents. SuperLambBanana (right) was created by Japanese artist Taro Chiezo as a parody of genetic engineering, while summer 2004 saw Penelope, the twisting, glowing steel sculpture by Cuban artist Jorge Pardo, arrive in Wolstenholme Square as a reference to both Liverpool's maritime past and the unshakable faith of Ulysses's wife in the ancient Greek myth.

On the right, shadow and light play upon surfaces of new buildings at Princes Dock. In the heart of Rope Walks is the Foundation for Arts and Creative Technologies or FACT (below left), the city's first purpose-built arts centre for more than 60 years and very different in character to the surrounding red-brick warehouses. The emphasis is upon transparency and public access, with cantilevered stairs inside and glazed facades looking out across the Liverpool cityscape. Throughout the building, the calm colours of natural materials provide a suitable backdrop for the art on display. Below right, the Royal Liver Building is reflected in the window panes of Beetham Plaza on the Strand opposite the Pier Head, and on the right, new and traditional methods of support as the former General Post Office on Victoria Street is transformed into the Met Quarter shopping centre, with its fabulous façade retained.

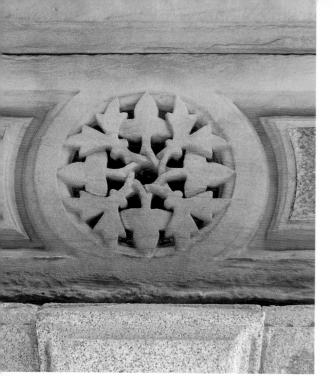

PALAZZO

The 150-year-old Albany on Old Hall Street is one of the jewels in Liverpool's crown of listed buildings, occupying almost an entire block and boasting a central courtyard with two spiral staircases. In the mid-19th century this area was the epicentre of the cotton trade, not just in Liverpool but in the world, and the Albany embodied the city's commercial might. It was built in 1858 for Richard Naylor, a banker and philanthropist, and it was used as both a meeting place for Liverpool's cotton brokers and storage space for their bales. The architect was J.K. Colling, a Londoner with a passion for flower drawing, who also designed the National Portrait Gallery near Trafalgar Square and whose lithographs from his book *Details of Gothic Architecture* are popular as posters today.

The initials of Richard Christopher Naylor are carved in a monogram upon the Albany's main entrance. A partner in his family's Liverpool bank Leyland & Bullins, he retired aged 34 when he and his brother inherited a fortune from their uncle in 1848. Before he built the Albany, he used his new-found wealth to buy Hooton Hall near Ellesmere Port from the Earls of Derby, who were forced to sell their hereditary home to pay off gambling debts. Naylor himself loved horse racing and in 1863 his own horse Macaroni won the Derby. He built a racecourse in the grounds of the hall that remained in use until 1914 when it was converted to barracks for the King's 18th Liverpool Rifles, then an airfield. Naylor died in 1899. A century later, in March 2002, his collection of racehorse paintings were auctioned by a descendant at Sotheby's. The 11 canvases by John Frederick Herring Snr, one of the most successful British equestrian artists of the 19th century, fetched over £300,000.

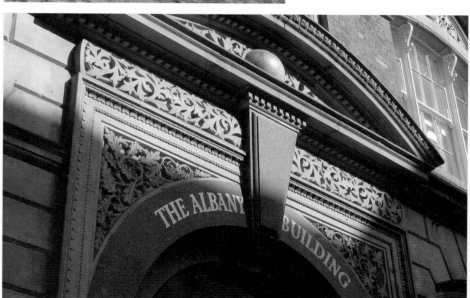

POST OFFICE

Now restored to its original, gleaming-white grandeur and re-opened as a shopping mall, the former GPO Building on Victoria Street has one of the finest sculptural façades in Liverpool. Allegorical figures in classical robes are seated with the royal coat of arms and maritime motifs, such as anchors, ropes and tillers, and cherubs hold up miniature columns surrounded by garlands, swags, torches and grotesque horned heads. In an arched niche between the columns is the winged helmet and caduceus (wand) of Mercury, the messenger god, accompanied by cornucopias of fruit and squirrels and birds perched on branches. Dating from the 1890s, the building was designed by Henry Tanner, the architect behind the slightly earlier London GPO. The sculptor was Edward O. Griffith, who would later produce the frieze along the exterior of the Cunard Building illustrating the shields of allied countries in World War One.

PUB

Not so much a public house as a work of genius, the Philharmonic Hotel at the corner of Hope Street and Mount Pleasant is as aesthetically pleasing as any civic building in Liverpool. Built in 1900 to the designs of Walter Thomas and the university's School of Art, it features wrought-iron and beaten-copper gates (left) and decorative stained glass (right) by ships' carpenters used to working on the interiors of transatlantic liners. The Lion Tavern at Moorfields (below), with its stained-glass domed skylight, is one

Music
is the
Universal
Language
of
Mankind
Longfellow

of local brewer Robert Cain's Victorian gems. Another, the splendidly-baroque Vines on Lime Street (left and right), has polished brass, mahogany caryatids (carved female figures serving as pillars) and an intricate zodiac upon the ceiling. It, too, was designed by Walter Thomas. The equally-ornate Doctor Duncans on St John's Lane (below) was named after Liverpool's first medical officer of health and occupies the old premises of Pearl Assurance. 'Liverpool is tremendously lucky to have a number of pubs which are outstanding in terms of their architecture and fittings', proclaims English Heritage in a recent guide to the country's hostelries. 'The Philharmonic and Vines are unmatched anywhere in the country for the opulence of their interiors.'

RELIC

Echoes of bygone Liverpool are found in the faded signs on the likes of Dublin Street near Stanley Dock (left), Copperas Hill (bottom left) and Roscoe Street (bottom right). On Fleet Street in Rope Walks – the area between Bold Street and Duke Street with one of the UK's largest concentrations of historic warehouses – a sign recalls the Victorian ropery industry. Overleaf is a sample of the hydraulic lifts once used to hoist goods and produce at the Albert Dock (main picture), Hackins Hey (top left), Sweeting Street (top right) and the Albany Building on Old Hall Street (bottom).

Liverpool's obsolete dockland furniture
includes drinking fountains like the one
near Salthouse Dock (right) and cast-iron
capstans (below left) and bollards (below
right), here both at the Albert Dock.
Consisting of circular drumheads (with
gears inside) above revolving barrels,
capstans were originally installed on ships then
on quaysides to manoeuvre the vessels. Often
set five feet below the surface, bollards were
designed to steer tethered boats through
narrow passages. The device behind the bollard
in the picture is a snatch head or idler wheel,
used to change the direction of the rope.
Standing proudly if somewhat incongruously
upon wasteground between Collingwood Dock
and Salisbury Dock is the Grade II listed,
hexagonal Victoria Tower (right). Built in 1848,
it not only gave the time to dock workers and
passing ships but also sounded high-tide
warnings with its bell – and repeated
the dockland fortress motif. Overleaf is an
iron plate on Cunliffe Street (off Tithebarn
Street) bearing the name of a local foundry,
which can be found upon many warehouses in
the city.

RIVER

The Mersey gives Liverpool its lyricism, and the sea gives the city its romance. 'A mile-wide stretch of muddy water – for the quality of Mersey is not strained – mirrors the weather of the day', observes city historian Quentin Hughes in his seminal 1960s book *Seaport*. 'Now deep, turgid and impenetrable like the cloak of encircling grey cloud, now sprightly dancing with tufts of white blown spray as the clear sky throws up a translucent brilliance which follows a northern wind.' The piture on the right shows it sparkling on a sunny day with the view towards the tunnel ventilation shaft in Birkenhead. On the far right is spume, captured through the powerful ropes and stout fairleads of a Mersey ferry. Overleaf shows it ebbing and flowing against the impervious Albert Dock seawall built by the legendary Jesse Hartley, and also seagulls perched upon the old landing stage at Princes Dock – once the embarkation point for millions of European emigrants to North America – watching the world and a ferry go by.

SHIELD

Liverpool's coat of arms, pictured here upon the former Exchange Station on Tithebarn Street (right), was granted in 1797 and depicts Neptune and a conch-blowing triton (a minor sea god) supporting a shield containing and surmounted by Liver Birds, or, more strictly, cormorants, 'in the beak a branch of seaweed called laver'. The motto *Deus Nobis Haec Otia Fecit* translates as 'These Gifts God Has Bestowed Upon Us.' Below left is an armorial shield on Ormond Street (off Old Hall Street), and below right are three Liver Birds around an open book on the university's arms. Bottom are the arms of the West Derby Hundred within the historic county of Lancaster, upon the County Sessions House on William Brown Street.

SPIRE

At the top of Brownlow Hill is Liverpool's own dreaming spire above the clocktower of the university's Victoria Building (below), designed by Alfred Waterhouse, master architect of Gothic Revival in the late-19th century.

On the right, zooming in upon the elaborately-decorated spire of the Municipal Buildings, now the city council's rates hall, on Dale Street. Note the ridge-backed reptiles with coiled tails clinging to the spire's sloping faces.

STAIRCASE

The cast-iron spiral staircase of 16 Cook Street (below), the narrow throughfare trundling down from Castle Street to Victoria Street, has 69 steps twisting from top to bottom through four storeys, and it is enclosed on the outside by a glass cylinder. The jewel in the crown of the Athenaeum on Church Alley is the elliptical (oval) staircase, which is the only one in Liverpool (right), curving elegantly up three floors to the library and reading room.

STATUE

No less than 16 large allegorical figures, representing indigenous peoples of the world and aspects of industry, technology, art and science, stand upon the second-storey ledges of the Municipal Buildings on Dale Street, erected in 1866. Navigation's hand rests upon a mermaid figurehead (below left), Electricity (below right) bears a star upon her head and holds thunderbolts, while Africa (right) wears a traditional costume and carries a bejewelled casket. Pictured overleaf are the various other figures with rich symbolic detailing, including Medicine (bottom right) leaning on the same kind of Hippocratic, serpent-entwined staff that appears upon the mosaic floor of the Medical Institution on Mount Pleasant.

165

Above the entrance to Lewis's department store, Liverpool Resurgent (left) dominates the nexus of five thoroughfares at Ranelagh Place. He was created in 1954 by Jacob Epstein (born in New York and studied with Rodin in Paris) to symbolise the city's indomitability after 68 air raids during World War Two, and he is known locally as Dickie Lewis, for fairly self-evident reasons. Below left, with his legs crossed, is the Scottish merchant and Liverpool MP William Ewart, in the Oratory near the Anglican Cathedral. Below right, the Victorian art collector and antiquarian Joseph Mayer strikes a noble pose in St George's Hall.

STREET

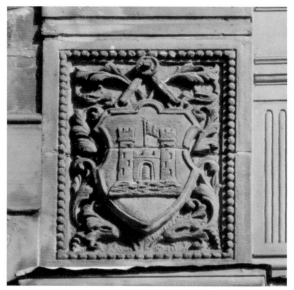

Castle Street, one of the city's seven ancient thoroughfares, was named after the medieval stronghold that once stood at its eastern end (the site of today's Victoria Monument) and survives in the sculptural details of several of its buildings. The architecture here is overwhelmingly Victorian, a reaction to the rapid growth of Liverpool's docks in the preceding century, with rows of elegant premises steeped in history. Wander along and the whiff of commerce hits you straightaway. From the rooftops, fabulous mermen and assorted mythological figures look down upon the street's busy traffic.

171

Bold Street marks a shift in the city-centre's character, a conduit from retail therapy to artsy bohemia. It's an urban village and tumult of activity, all crowds and multilingual chatter, buskers and specialist stores, charismatic cafés and delis on a thoroughfare once compared with London's Bond Street. The evidence is in the architecture, which is as eclectic as anywhere in the city with late

Georgian, mock Florentine and art deco façades signifying the former premises of gentlemen's tailors, hair salons, concert halls and tea rooms. Between here and Duke Street is the Rope Walks district, one of the largest concentrations of historic warehouses in the whole country, criss-crossed with lively squares, small gardens and walkways, and blessed with 90 listed buildings some dormant, many revitalised.

Water Street is Liverpool's mightiest and most enduring thoroughfare – voted one of the country's five favourite streets by BBC Radio Four's *Today* programme. History resonates along its grand incline, from the Town Hall to the waterfront, and breakthroughs in modern architecture have also found a foothold here. 'The city is built high, in a way reminiscent of her American sisters', wrote Liverpool urban historian Quentin Hughes. 'The height is most evident in the office blocks of Water Street and the sheer rising walls which climb into the sky before we reach the windswept plateau of the Pier Head.' Overleaf are the street's adjacent glass palaces of Oriel Chambers, designed as early as 1864 by Peter Ellis, and the much later Norwich House.

TEMPLE

Grade I listed and described in one official guidebook as 'the ultimate in civic pride, deliberately proportioned to be bigger and better than any public building in the land', St George's Hall occupies a commanding position upon a natural outcrop of sandstone in what was envisaged as the 'forum' of Liverpool by the city's Victorian elite. This 490ft long, neoclassical masterpiece was designed by 23-year-old Harvey Lonsdale Elmes as an emphatic declaration of the city's status as the second city of the British Empire.

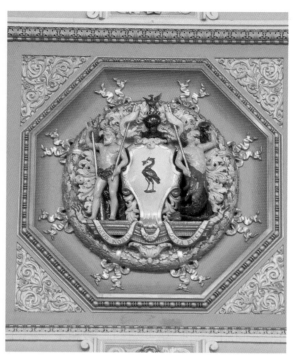

On a tour of Liverpool in 1851, Queen Victoria said it was 'worthy of ancient Athens, the architecture is so simple and magnificent'. It has a 7,737-pipe organ, an exquisite sunken floor covered with blue and brown Minton tiles and it has stained-glass windows at either end depicting Liverpool's coat of arms and St George and the Dragon. The arms reappear upon the vaulted celing (left), and on the six pairs of bronze doors inside are the letters SPQL (below), an adaptation of the motto of Rome and meaning 'to the Senate and the People of Liverpool'. Along the east façade of the hall, either side of the main entrance, are two sets of six reliefs between 1885 and 1901, entitled The Progress of Justice (right) and National Prosperity. The nude figures caused a scandal in their day. In 2006 they were cleaned and restored to their original splendor.

TERRACE

On the brow of the big city sit rows of handsome Georgian properties on cobbled, tree-lined streets. This was the address of Liverpool's most affluent citizens in the 19th century, and today it's still a leafy retreat from the city centre as well as a hotbed of arts and academia, blending seamlessly into the main university campus with great views down to the Pier Head. Pictured left and right are the windows and terraces on Falkner Street. Below is Canning Street and overleaf is an excellent period house on Mount Pleasant.

Today the Georgian terraces of Rodney Street are home to physiotherapists, acupuncturists and dental surgeons. But they're also an historical who's who of the city. James Maury, the first US consul in Liverpool, lived at no. 4 from 1790 to 1829. Nos. 9, 11, 34 and 62 were the respective birthplaces of poet Arthur Clough, author Nicholas Monsarrat, Henry Booth (founder of the Liverpool & Manchester Railway) and William Gladstone (four times Prime Minister). At no. 59 (below), the home of photographer Edward Chambre-Hardman has been converted into a museum. Over 140,000 of his images are displayed in a 1940s interior. Overleaf is another fine, three-storey property on Bedford Street South.

Falkner Square (below) is bucolic and historic. A blue plaque at no. 40 commemorates the erstwhile home of Liverpool architect Peter Ellis, who designed the Grade I listed, glass-and-stone ensemble of Oriel Chambers on Water Street. In the 1860s, merchant James Spence lived at no. 32. A staunch fundraiser for the southern states during the American Civil War, Spence even lobbied parliament to recognise their status. The square was named after Edward Falkner, a *Boy's–Own* hero who mustered a fighting force of 1,000 men when a French invasion threatened the country in 1797. Canning Street (far right), together with Percy Street, Huskisson Street (right) and Gambier Terrace, comprises a conservation area of late Georgian housing with columned porches and grand balconies. Once home to Liverpool's gentry, it is regularly commandeered by camera crews for period dramas.

TOWN HALL

It's handsome enough when approached from Castle Street upon a floodlit evening, but the best view of Liverpool's Town Hall is arguably from the rear, most certainly on a summer's evening when the setting sun bathes the statues of the Four Seasons in a soft glow above the cobbled stage of the Exchange Flags (the city's original cotton exchange). Higher still, Athena/Minerva (left), the Greek/Roman goddess of wisdom, presides over Liverpool from the dome above. One of Liverpool's Georgian gems, this is the third Town Hall to stand on this site and dates from the late-18th century.

VIEW

Pictured left is the waterfront from Wallasey, and below is the view up St John's Lane with St George's Hall in the background. At the bottom is the city centre from Heyworth Street, and on the right a ferry passing the Graces. Overleaf is the dome of the Town Hall and city skyline.

WALL

Running alongside Liverpool's docks for the best part of six miles is the fortress-like, Grade II listed Boundary Wall, rising 18ft high in places and punctuated by colossal gatepiers. The novelist Nathaniel Hawthorne, an American consul in Liverpool in the 1850s, likened it to the Great Wall of China. The red-brick section near the Princes Dock (below) dates back to 1816. Thirty years later, dock engineer Jesse Hartley extended the wall in irregular granite (right) to control access to and from the docks. Large slabs built into the outer wall are carved with both the names of the docks behind and the date of their completion.

WAREHOUSE

Few of Liverpool's mighty warehouses survive today. Two at Waterloo Dock were demolished just after the war and in 1969 respectively. The remaining five-storey building (right) has as much floorspace as all of the Albert Dock warehouses (below) put together. On the far right is the majestic Wapping Dock warehouse. Overleaf are windows framed by multi-coloured brick on Cheapside, near Dale Street in the city centre.

Tall warehouses from the late-Victorian period are still crammed along narrow, sloping thoroughfares like Bridgwater Street (below) and Watkinson Street (far right), framed by Parliament Street and Jamaica Street near the south docks. They are characterised by stacked loading bays for each floor that were once served by hoists and pulleys, with the dates of their construction invariably marked in stone plaques or iron plates under the gable. On the right are midday motes of sunshine upon warehouse loading bays on Davies Street, off Dale Street.

Pictured on the previous page, the cast-iron columns of a derelict warehouse on Stanley Dock, north of the Pier Head, mirror those of the Albert Dock. This building was used to store coal from canal barges. The gargantuan tobacco warehouse (this page) on the opposite side of Stanley Dock arrived later in the 19th century and reputedly contains 27 million bricks. Resolutely utilitarian and uncompromising, but magnificent nonetheless. Overleaf is another giant on Jamaica Street.

ZODIAC

Under a horoscopic lens, the last and most beautiful of the Three Graces reveals a dozen sculptural secrets. Most observers are familiar with the Cunard Building's monumental entrances, with their stone stairs, panelled oak doors, bronze lamps and fluted columns, as well the massive eagles protruding from each corner and the heads of exotic peoples from all over the world running along its sides. Less may have noticed the signs of the zodiac, too: from the swaddled twin babes of Gemini to the bow and arrow quiver of Sagittarius, all worked in enduring Portland stone. These are, after all, on the erstwhile headquarters of a great shipping line with its origins firmly in Liverpool, and astrology was an ancient tool for navigation, so their appearance in consecutive roundels upon the building does have meaning. Overleaf, the 12 signs as they also appear high upon the elevations of the earlier Exchange Station on Tithebarn Street (comic-book eyes upon the scorpion notwithstanding). Along with figures from classical mythology, the signs of the zodiac have been a common feature of decorative sculpture in Europe since Renaissance times, side by side with more conventional religious imagery despite their obvious pagan connotations.

214

ZOO

A camel on Ranelagh Street (left), a squirrel gathering nuts on Mathew Street (below) and a pheasant at Haymarket (right) are just some of the menagerie on display in the city centre. Bottom is another camel and an elephant on the Town Hall. Pictured overleaf are hunter and prey in carved reliefs along the former Fruit Exchange on Victoria Street.

RECOMMENDED READING

Of the many excellent publications celebrating Liverpool and its architecture, three in particular warrant special mention as authoritative guides and invaluable reference sources:

Pevsner Architectural Guides: Liverpool
Joseph Sharples (Pevsner, 2004)

Public Sculpture of Liverpool
Terry Cavanagh (Liverpool University Press, 1997)

Seaport: Architecture & Townscape in Liverpool
Quentin Hughes (Bluecoat Press, 1993)